What _Would_ Jesus Do? A Handbook

How would the Son of Man deal with some of the problems facing you and me today?

by
Michael Meier

1663 LIBERTY DRIVE, SUITE 200
BLOOMINGTON, INDIANA 47403
(800) 839-8640
WWW.AUTHORHOUSE.COM

© 2003, 2004 Michael Meier
All Rights Reserved.

No part of this book may be reproduced, stored in a retrieval system, or transmitted by any means without the written permission of the author.

First published by AuthorHouse 11/24/04

ISBN: 1-4184-9217-5 (sc)

Printed in the United States of America
Bloomington, Indiana

This book is printed on acid-free paper.

Contents

Preface vi
1. Why We Need This Book 1
2. An Example of Faith 13
3. Responsibility To God 19
4. Responsibility To Others 26
5. Responsibility To Family 39
6. Responsibility To Ourselves 43
7. Possessions 47
8. Wealth 52
9. A Challenge 56
10. Applications 60
    10.1. Homosexuality 61
    10.2. Abortion 64
    10.3. Poverty, Hunger, Disease 67
11. The Way, The Truth, The Life 70
12. The Bottom Line 72
13. Origins 75
Postscript 80
Questions for Discussion and Thought 85

Preface

The Holy Bible is a wonderful book. It contains everything we should ever need to know about the mind of God and the faith journey. We should begin our journey in the Bible and we should end it there.

I will hope for but not expect to fully experience God in this life. I am peaceful in the assurance that I will do so in the next life. Until then, the best I can do is to reflect on my own contacts with God and seek to enter into the contacts of others by experiencing them second-hand.

Many people have difficulty relating to the Bible because the stories in it take place thousands of years ago. Although it is both interesting and comforting to recognize in biblical characters traits that we see every day, we may still feel a sense of distance because of the settings and the language.

How do you feel about the Bible? Have you read it? Do you read it? Why or why not?

Latter-day experiences may be more accessible to us because we have an easier time relating to conditions and outcomes. In other words, by reading about (for example) my experiences in the present time, you may find it easier to place yourself within the experience and use it to further develop your own relationship with God.

Begin with the Bible. End with the Bible. Remember that God is working in people's lives today in real, though not provable, ways. We want to share with you. In any group, ask the question, "How has God touched your life?" You'll be surprised at the response.

I have left space at the bottom of each page for your use. My thought was that I might wish to make notes to myself or document my feelings as I read. I have recently been introduced to the idea of a reading journal. This is simply a journal of one's thoughts and reactions to whatever is being read.

Which Biblical person do you know best? Why?

In my own life, I recognize that I would hardly ever be prepared with what I needed to do this kind of journaling, even though I have found it to be a wonderful way to experience a book or story.

For all who might have the same difficulty, all you will need is a flat pen or pencil to use as a bookmark. With this handy, you have everything you need for journaling.

Why might it be a good idea to journal?

1. Why We Need This Book

Why should I care what Jesus would do?

Do you really think it's possible to know what a person of 2000 years ago would do in today's world?

What good will it do me to know what Jesus would do? Jesus was God and the Son of God so how can I hope to do what he would do?

On one level, knowing how Jesus would act in our own situation is a way to tap into and use the wisdom that Jesus possessed. On this level Jesus may be considered a symbol, a standard, an ideal. It does absolutely no good to ask what Jesus would do if we can't come up with an answer we can have confidence in.

The past few years have seen something of a fad involving Jesus. It has become popular in schools, in work settings and even in Hollywood, to wear something displaying the letters **WWJD**.

Why do you care what Jesus would do?

Michael Meier

The purpose, as most people understand it, is to remind the person wearing the bracelet or necklace or key ring or T-shirt or whatever to always ask himself or herself. "What would Jesus do?" and, by doing so, make better decisions for their own lives.

This kind of reminder can be effective if the wearer is sincere. If the wearer is only being "in" or is wearing the symbol just because everyone else is, then the question has no power.

People have always worn symbols for their decorative value, often without even knowing that their decoration has meaning. Sometimes the wearer might be aware that the symbol has meaning for others, but may display it anyway.

Some symbols are held in private. I might carry a small cross inscribed with the words, "God loves you."

What symbols are important to you? Why?

What _Would_ Jesus Do?

I have carried such a cross in my pocket for its value to me as a reminder. Every time I put my hand in my pocket, I thought of that message. From time to time, I have met someone who needed that message for himself or for someone else. I have given that symbol away to someone who needed it.

I had some small heart-shaped appliqués made, red with a white cross in the middle. I sewed them onto some of my shirt cuffs. These were and are a reminder to me to "wear my heart on my sleeve."

Symbols meant to reflect a relationship with Jesus require an understanding of the personality and character of Jesus if they are to be effective in guiding us through life's pitfalls.

Such an understanding comes into our heart/our soul with the Holy Spirit. At the moment we accept the gift of salvation from Jesus, we know Him.

Why might it be a good idea to understand the symbols you display?

Michael Meier

OK, you might be saying, but if I know Him, why do I need this handbook? I believe we need this for the same reason that we need books about successful marriage relationships or raising children.

I know my spouse and my children very well, so why do I sometimes make such huge blunders in relating to them? In my most honest moments, I understand that it's because I don't look for opportunities to practice what I know to be the most loving relationship behaviors. Then, when the opportunity finds me, I am simply not prepared to respond in the best way. We know what to do, but in the heat of the moment, it's all too easy to forget.

By practicing loving behaviors—even when they aren't "required"—I can make it more likely that in a time of stress I will naturally and effectively respond out of love.

By reading and rereading these helpful relationship handbooks, we can ingrain these productive responses into our character so that when the heat is turned up, our first response has a much better chance of being the right one.

Does "practice make perfect"?

What *Would* Jesus Do?

It's almost trite to say that we live in an age of unprecedented challenges to our faith.

It seems people have been saying that since David, Ezekiel, Jeremiah, and Elijah. The fact is that each and every new day, each new person we meet, each new situation presents a challenge to faith.

In matters of faith, the fact that others have experienced this particular challenge and have fallen or triumphed is only relevant if we are aware of that victory or defeat. In other words, if we don't know about it, we can't use it.

That said, it becomes painfully obvious that cultivating faith must mean becoming aware of the faith struggles of others. The intent of this handbook is to prepare a person of faith with tools designed to build, nurture, protect and enhance faith throughout a lifetime.

Who are your role models?

Michael Meier

For those who do not yet know what faith involves, my hope and prayer is that you will experience faith here and so come to gain an understanding of what a life in faith may require (and will deliver). You will see that it won't be easy. In fact, it may be impossible for us to live the life described by Jesus.

You see, it is not possible to define faith in any way that is meaningful. A dictionary can give us a framework but it isn't very helpful in getting us to where we need to be. If I say that faith is action based on belief, it simply stimulates more questions. Belief in what? What kind of action?

Language is a tool for dissecting a procedure or an object and then putting it back together in another way so that it becomes more useful.

But for some things language and words become the most useless of tools. Even describing a cloud or flower is frequently beyond the reach of any set of words. When this problem comes up, we create an album of word pictures to communicate a single feeling or thought.

When do you resort to stories to describe something? Are they effective?

What *Would* Jesus Do?

When Jesus used stories or parables, this is what he was doing. Faith isn't something to be defined in a few words or a few sentences. It will take many words arranged and rearranged to begin to communicate the idea of what Jesus had in mind (or in heart) when he spoke of faith.

He found that he needed different stories for different people and situations. A single story can't provide the kind of understanding needed to live a life in faith.

The beginning of the Christian era in the lands at the eastern end of the Mediterranean required examples based on tending flocks, growing grapes, making wine, fishing, and living as subjects of an occupying power. The details of the stories are not important. Rather it is the faith and love of which the stories tell that is important.

What does faith require?

Michael Meier

In all humility, I have set myself the task (or, more correctly, God has given me the task) of extracting the message that Jesus delivered from the stories and "re-issuing" it for our own time. My experience has been that trying to grasp the historical implications and the details of life in the land of Israel under Roman rule frequently distracts from the real message.

I have on occasion asked myself whether we have received the true word of God through all of the translating and political maneuvering that has produced the various versions of the Bible that we use today. My conclusion is that God's message is still there, but we must work harder to extract it. The Church (of whatever denomination) has been so conservative and literal in approving new translations, that the message may be, if anything, more difficult to understand today than it was 2000 years ago.

Is it important that we are reading translations when we read the Bible? Why or why not?

What *Would* Jesus Do?

I have done some translating of German and Russian into English. My approach, which is the same as that of all translators, is to capture the sense and style of the work. The object of translation is to communicate the message of the work to a new audience. Do modern Bible translations do this? The politics of producing a new translation and getting it approved by committees and denominations practically guarantees that preservation of sense and style takes a back seat in negotiations about the use of this word versus that one.

You will note that, while I make reference to Biblical events, I do not give book, chapter, or verse. I do this for all of the reasons alluded to above and one more. Much of the difficulty we experience with the Bible stems from our unwillingness to consider the Bible's story more than a "bite" at a time.

Chapter and verse numbering was added to the bible in the 16th century in order to make it easier to refer to specific thoughts or ideas contained in it. This is no different than turning on line numbering in a word processing program. It is also no more meaningful. Chapter and verse are conventions to aid us but which would have meant nothing to the authors

What's your experience with "sound bites"?

Michael Meier

When a verse or part of a verse is pulled out as a "sound bite" its meaning can be changed significantly. An example that comes immediately to mind is Matthew 4:6, a frequently quoted fragment of a verse. "...'He shall give His angels charge over you', and, 'In their hands they shall bear you up, Lest you dash your foot against a stone.'" (NKJV)

There are two problems here. The first is that this is actually a quote from Old Testament scripture (Psalm 91:11, 12). The second is that the individual who was quoting this scripture was a devil who was using this to tempt Jesus to jump from the pinnacle of the temple in Jerusalem.

Lifting this passage and referring to its source as Matthew, makes it seem like part of the Gospel and may even leave the impression that it was Jesus who was speaking these words. Certainly, the entire context of temptation is lost as is Jesus' reply.

My rule of thumb is:

Never accept a sound bite–even one from the Bible–at face value.

What insights did you receive from your most recent reading of the Bible?

What *Would* Jesus Do?

This rule is a good one to include in a handbook like this. It will keep us from falling victim to the temptation to judge our neighbor. Devils come in many disguises.

The tabloid press uses out-of-context quotations to create sensation. Reputable news media use them to try to give a sense of what was said while eliminating the *fluff*. Is your definition of *fluff* the same as the reporter's? Is the reporter's or editor's the same as that of the original speaker?

Political partisans use out-of-context quotes to make the opponent into a devil. Advertisers, who take one or two words or a phrase and put them into an entirely different context, frequently victimize book and movie reviewers. This has been done so blatantly and so frequently that it has become a joke.

So, because meaning can be so easily lost or hidden, I will refrain from giving references here except to refer to an entire story. When we use the Bible, we should use it in pieces that tell an entire story.

Have you been more often disappointed or excited when you found out the whole story?

Michael Meier

Rev. James Ross, an Elder of the United Methodist Church, advised me to pray before I read my Bible, asking God to grant me insight from what I read. This is an excellent practice.

It is also worthwhile for those who are interested in a particular story referenced here to use readily available resources to look up the story. Excellent on-line resources are accessible such as

www.biblegateway.com

which allows keyword searching of the entire Bible and will present text in any of more than a dozen different English translations.

What might be learned from comparing two or more different English translations?

2. An Example of Faith

I don't understand what faith is or how to know whether I have it.

I can't put faith ahead of the demands of my job.

How can I bring faith into my relationship with my spouse?

Faith just doesn't seem to fit today. How can I make faith meaningful today?

Jesus, the Christ, son of Mary, Son of God, must be the first exemplar of faith. He is the One who said, "I am the way, the truth and the life."

This statement is the boldest, strongest statement of faith that I can imagine.

What do you think of "I am the Way..." as a statement of faith?

Michael Meier

Mohandas K. Gandhi, known as *the Mahatma* (a title of respect for a person venerated for great knowledge and love of humanity), said, "We must be the change that we wish to see in the world."

Gandhi, who was a Hindu, believed in God and in Truth, which he viewed as a manifestation of God. His faith moved two mountains—the population of India and the British Empire. And yet, his statement is second to that of Jesus.

In his statement of faith, Gandhi admitted to himself that he sometimes may not be that change. Indeed, he never made a claim to perfection. He was exhorting himself to strive to be the way, the truth and the life.

His statement was a symbol that he carried in his head, in his heart, and in his soul, to remind him of what he must do.

We would do well to attain Gandhi's faith, whether as Christian, Hindu, Muslim, Buddhist or Jew. But I hope it is as clear to you as it is to me that Jesus represents a huge step up in terms of faith.

Do you see a difference between " I am" and "I must be"?
How do you understand the difference?

What *Would* Jesus Do?

Even characters in popular fiction can give us help in our faith walk. For example, Yoda, the Jedi master, told Luke Skywalker during a training session that, "There is no *try*. There is only *do* or not *do*."

In light of Yoda's advice, we can see that Gandhi was still contending with *not do*. He frequently crossed over to the side of *do* as witnessed by the incredible effect of his life on hundreds of millions of people. Yet he, himself, understood that he had not achieved the level of faith that was necessary. His use of *must* ("We *must* be the change …") shows an imperfect level of attainment.

Jesus, on the other hand, did not even allow for the possibility of *try* or *not do*. *I am* is a statement of perfection. Jesus was clearly equipped with the faith to *do*.

Even more powerfully, his statement reflects a lack of concern for *do*ing. He tells us that as the way, the truth and the life, doing is, if not completely irrelevant, then at best unimportant. *Do*ing is of the world, while *be*ing transcends the world.

What insights did you receive from your most recent reading of the Bible?

Michael Meier

We can see from examples in the gospels how much Jesus respected this kind of faith—faith that held no concern for what to do, but was completely focused on being.

- The centurion who wished only for Jesus' assurance of healing

- Mary, who sat at his feet content to be in his presence, while Martha concerned herself with all of the doing

- the woman "who had led a sinful life" washed the feet of Jesus with her tears and dried them with her hair

- Mary, the sister of Lazarus, who anointed the feet of Jesus with costly perfume and dried them with her hair

Imagine if Jesus had said, "I'm doing the best I can to be the Way..."? Your thoughts?

What _Would_ Jesus Do?

These are examples of *being* that confused those witnesses who were blinded by the *doing*. Because the acts themselves (doing) seemed so out of the ordinary, they became the cause of confusion for bystanders. However, Jesus, who saw the being, simply accepted the acts and focused on the faith.

In all situations, with all people, in all of life, hold the example of Jesus in your heart. Be the Way, the Truth, and the Life.

Practice this way:

- *Close your eyes and become conscious of yourself.*

- *When you are quiet, become aware of the strongest feeling of love within you.*

- *Let this love become larger until it is greater than you and includes the others in your world.*

- *Now feel the immensely greater love of which your love is but a part.*

- *Let the love of God surround you, envelope you, and bring you into the heart of God.*

- *Pause and be cleansed and renewed within God's heart. Feel the safety and the power here.*

Do you feel God? How? When?

Michael Meier

- *Reach out your hand and touch Jesus. He's right there next to you.*

- *Merge with Jesus. Become Jesus. Put him on like a robe.*

- *Become the Way, the Truth, and the Life there in the security and strength of God's heart.*

- *Feel what it means to be the Way, the Truth, and the Life. Let yourself linger and absorb.*

- *Now, still one with Jesus, allow yourself to come back. Stay in contact with God's heart and come gently back to this world.*

- *When you are ready, go into the world as the Way, the Truth, and the Life for the others you meet.*

What does it mean to you to "be the way, the truth and the life"?

3. Responsibility To God

What does God expect of me?

How can I ever be the person God wants me to be?

What if I don't give God what he wants?

What do we owe to God?

Jesus was very clear on this. We are to love the Lord God with all our heart and soul and mind and strength.

God does not ask for anything. We freely offer everything out of love. Gratitude is the only thing we have to offer that can acknowledge the supreme generosity and grace of what God has given us.

What do you feel responsible for?

Michael Meier

Just as in human interactions, to try to reciprocate a gift given from the heart is to make it less. When a child comes excitedly to mother or father with the hand painted plaster cast of her hand or the carefully drawn and colored picture of a family activity, no response is appropriate other than, "Thank you. I love you."

Children know this but adults have forgotten. When I give something to a child, they don't immediately feel guilty because they have nothing to give me in return. They will say things that mean thank you. "I can't believe you did that for me." "Will you share it with me?"

Does God need my money? My time? My adoration? Why do we get confused about this? God certainly has no need of money nor of time nor of worship. God needs nothing. God has no need. But if God has no need then on what do we base our responsibility to Him? All of the direction provided by God to his children throughout history has had but one aim–to bring prosperity, joy and peace to the children.

Is "thank you" the best response? Why or why not?

What *Would* Jesus Do?

What is your children's responsibility to you as parent? Our children sometimes asked us, "What should we do?" Sometimes one would even say, "What do you want me to do?" Our answer was always the same–we wanted them to be happy, be in a loving relationship, find peace–any advice or rules that we might provide were directed at those ends.

We are to seek first the Kingdom of God, but how many know that? How many fewer grasp what it means? When all of God's children are seeking His Kingdom, we will have the peace, joy, and prosperity that He intends for us.

Wouldn't your children's lives be better, easier, less frustrating and more productive if they would only listen to and obey the loving rules their parents have provided? Do your children say, "But I want to do it this way." (Or do you say this to your parents?)

Seeking the Kingdom is a cooperative effort. We are all aware that the Kingdom is out there. We feel the lack of it in our lives.

Compare your relationship with your children to God relationship with you? How are you doing?

Michael Meier

Our need is to be close to God and to be in faith that the world will be best realized as God's Kingdom. When that is our faith, then we will act in that faith. That action, rooted in faith, is our only responsibility.

Then one day, we get a clue. Someone starts us out on the search. Others, recognizing that we are now searching, offer the help that they are qualified to provide.

We begin to see the love and gratitude offered by others. Then we begin to see the reason for the love and gratitude. One day, one instant, we suddenly see, feel, experience, the gift of God's grace and we enter into the Kingdom.

At this point, we become one of those who offers to others the help that we are qualified to provide. We are vigilant and take our responsibility seriously. The very focus of our life changes. We try to better understand our own gift(s) so that we may understand better how to use them in guiding others.

Can you love without giving? Can you be in a relationship with God without loving?

What *Would* Jesus Do?

In this, we may get the wrong idea. We may begin to feel responsible for bringing others to God. We may feel inadequate before that task and so shrink from it. The feelings of inadequacy generate the fear that we aren't "good enough" for God's Kingdom. †

We may lose the connection to God that was gratitude and love. We begin to see God as demanding, angry, retributive, vengeful, much as we sometimes see our biological or adoptive parents. *All of this happens because **we try** to take on more responsibility than we can handle.*

One day as I was crossing a street, I found myself next to a man who was reading a newspaper as he walked. The street was divided by a median. As we crossed the median, the man next to me did not look up from his newspaper. Either he was using me as a guide or he was on autopilot.

---

† Wild at Heart by John Eldredge, 2001, Thomas Nelson Publishers, Nashville, for an in-depth discussion of our feelings of inadequacy.

How good do you have to be to fit into the Kingdom of God?

Michael Meier

As we prepared to step out into the traffic lane on the far side of the median, I noticed a cement truck approaching at a speed that would not allow it to stop before the crosswalk. I stopped, unwilling to challenge the truck for the right-of-way. The man next to me, still reading his newspaper, kept moving.

Without thinking, I assumed responsibility for his life and put out my arm to block his way. He looked up from his reading just as the truck roared by. He blinked, looked around as though waking up, then glanced at me and said, "Thanks." To the best of my knowledge, we never met again.

Afterward, I thought, "I saved his life." This happened many years ago, during a time in my life when I had lost that connection with God. I had experienced all of the inadequacy, fear, resentment that I described above. I couldn't see myself bringing people to God on their knees and I believed that was the only way to fulfill my obligation.

The incident in the crosswalk was given to me as a gift in order to demonstrate to me that whatever I was capable of was enough.

Have you saved a life? What did it mean?

What *Would* Jesus Do?

People save lives in momentous and spectacular and courageous ways and they are called heroes. Many more save lives in small, mundane and seemingly inconsequential ways. Those who are saved may not even notice them.

Clearly then, there can be no doubt as to what is expected of a person seeking God's Kingdom. In short, we need not worry about doing Christ-like things—acting like a Christian. Simply <u>be</u> Christ, approaching life in gratitude and love. Be a <u>Christ-ian</u> and all else will follow very naturally.

Love the Lord God with all your heart and with all your soul and with all your mind and with all your strength. This love will manifest in continuous gratitude and the joy that accompanies love.

How do you understand the difference between "doing" and "being"?

4. Responsibility To Others

I just don't get that 'love your neighbor' stuff. I barely even know my neighbor.

Who should I love?

Why should I love my neighbor? What's in it for me?

Here, again, Jesus left no doubt–no ambiguity. "Love your neighbor as yourself." The story that Jesus told to illustrate this makes it clear that we are to make neighbors of everyone by being a neighbor. Stated in another and maybe more appropriate way—being a neighbor creates neighbors. We are to give whatever mercy is within our power.

For whom do you feel responsible?

What *Would* Jesus Do?

What do we do as a neighbor and to whom do we do it? This question distracted the Pharisee to whom Jesus related the parable of the Good Samaritan. Jesus made it blindingly clear that it is our responsibility to <u>*create*</u> neighbors.

Everyone we meet must be a neighbor. Everyone we <u>don't</u> meet must be a neighbor.

Let's move on then to the follow-up question: "How do we make someone our neighbor?" Jesus gave an example of an act of a neighbor, but most of us find it all too easy to accept the most narrow of interpretations based on that example.

Many states have so-called "good samaritan laws" on the books. These laws demonstrate the narrow interpretation of the parable. They require a passer-by to render aid at the scene of an accident.

Surely, this is a good thing and something we would all want to do, but is it enough? There should be no doubt that Jesus had in mind something far more humble and at the same time far more grand. Even the Pharisee lawyer seemed to get it. When I *am* a neighbor to everyone, then everyone is my neighbor.

How might "love your neighbor" work in your community, the nation, the world?

Michael Meier

Love your neighbor as yourself. This love will manifest as acceptance, forgiveness and peace. The seeker will have already experienced personal peace and will now be sharing that peace with all to whom he is a neighbor.

We can see what our responsibility is to others. Jesus illuminated this responsibility with many examples to show us how we are expected to love our neighbor as we love ourselves.

As Jesus told that other Pharisee lawyer, the second most important law is "like unto" the first part. Our responsibility to others, then, is part of our responsibility to God.

God cannot be said to have expectations. God *is* ("I am") and furthermore, God *is* outside of time. When considering God, it simply makes no sense to speak of His expectations of us.

God did however make us and he made us perfect, in his image. In this light, we may accept the instruction of Jesus as a roadmap. If we would seek the Kingdom of God, we must follow the map.

God has no expectations. What is your response to this statement?

What *Would* Jesus Do?

The essence of neighboring is responsibility. First of all, a neighbor is aware. As a neighbor, we notice what is happening or not happening around us. I see the needs of my neighbor.

As we discussed earlier, when I am being a neighbor, I do my best to make sure things are taken care of. I do this in faith that in my need, a neighbor will be there.

In accepting this responsibility, I do not meddle in my neighbor's life. The things that I do as a neighbor do not require theological training. They do not require direction from someone with an advanced degree or some impressive credentials. They are simply the things that present themselves as obvious needs–needs that, if unmet, would mean harm to my neighbor.

What needs do your neighbors have that you could do something about?

Michael Meier

My rule of thumb here is that if there is *any* doubt that my neighbor would be grateful for my action, then I must forebear. In such cases, I might speak with him or her (or someone else) and discuss my impulse so as to try to understand what I should do or not do in future situations.

Two trivial but revealing examples will illustrate. I am always amazed at the number of people who would not stop a stranger to gently tell her that the tags of her clothing are hanging out at the neckline. Now it may be that people simply don't notice, but even that is un-neighborly. We should notice others.

If you are male, you have at some time found your fly open and wondered how long it had been that way. Very few would ever lean over and quietly tell a man that his fly is open. Yet, if it were your fly, wouldn't you prefer that the first person to notice would do something so that you didn't walk around for hours in disarray?

What are some more examples of everyday acts of love that you could or should or do perform?

What *Would* Jesus Do?

In the Kingdom, this is the way people relate to one another—in love and faith—responsibly. When we live in gratitude and in love, we are alert to any opportunity to pass those feelings on to others. We want everyone to feel as we do. We don't want to be in the Kingdom alone—its sole resident.

You may know someone who feels that he or she is entitled to heaven and is making it a life's work to keep out all those of lesser worth. This person is not in the Kingdom. Rather they are in their own little hell and fail to understand that no one is trying to get past them.

The Kingdom of God is not exclusive. <u>All</u> who wish to enter are welcomed.

It would seem then, that if we are taking care of our responsibilities to God, we are taking care of our responsibilities to others at the same time. In fact, if we consider for a moment we will see that "neighbors" and "others" are the same.

The gospel accounts are full of stories in which people come to Jesus or Jesus encounters someone. In every case, Jesus immediately accepted responsibility for their well being. He immediately became a neighbor.

What is your understanding of the "Kingdom of God"? How will you enter?

Michael Meier

The needs of these people included hunger, demons, disease, self-image, deadly peril and sin. In each case, Jesus responded at a very personal level to His neighbor in need. They left in a state of well being.

It is noteworthy that Jesus seems always to respond to *needs* rather than *wants*. We don't find stories of wants in the gospel accounts. It seems that we will find a way to satisfy our wants on our own, without any help. Our needs, on the other hand, *require* outside help. As a human, I need to be acknowledged. I need to be valued. I need to feel secure. My body needs food, water and oxygen.

People, our neighbors, can with God's help, provide us with some of these needs, but not very reliably and often not very effectively. When we have a relationship with God, however, all of these needs are satisfied. Please note, too, that God will satisfy these needs for anyone. After all, the rain falls alike on the just and the unjust. We all breathe the same air. The earth brings forth its bounty for all.

What are your desires? What are your needs?

What *Would* Jesus Do?

We owe it to our neighbor to be aware of him and to be aware of her condition. When we recognize our own essential helplessness, we are much more willing and able to take responsibility for the condition of our neighbor. Being responsible doesn't mean paying the rent or buying the groceries (although it could). Being responsible means living the golden rule.

In day-to-day living, we tend to look for the dramatic. We can readily see the big, dramatic opportunities to be a neighbor. Unfortunately for you and me and the Kingdom, while we are looking far and wide for opportunities to be a hero, there are tens, hundreds, thousands of needs that are going unmet right under our eyes.

What opportunities will you have today to save a life?

Michael Meier

When we stay behind that slow moving truck at the crest of a hill or in that curvy section of highway, we may well be saving someone's life. When we understand that we are dependent on someone else to protect us in that way, we are eager to return the favor. When we are standing at a corner with a mother and her small child and we choose to give the child a good example by waiting for the walk signal even though no traffic is coming, we may very well be saving a life.

It is precisely these small opportunities to be a neighbor that are the genuinely important ones. I need look no farther than my own relationship with my wife to validate this. She works hard at being a mother and a wife and she asks for very little. Yet she has a need for validation, acknowledgement, and appreciation. I know that as little as two or three thank-yous a day would be enough to make a huge difference in how she feels about herself. It is infinitely sad when we don't see the need for that tiny investment until it is too late.

What will you do to bring the Kingdom to someone today?

What *Would* Jesus Do?

If two or three thank-yous are enough for a spouse, it would require less than one per day for a coworker, an acquaintance, a stranger. In the workplace, if I make it a point to compliment or to thank everyone I interact with, I become known as "that really nice guy." If several people were doing this with me, the glow would transfer from us as individuals to the workplace in general. "This is a great place to work."

I have one more personal story that seems to fit here, although the lessons go beyond our interactions with neighbors. I was driving with my wife and son in the car with me. It was in that last half-hour before dark and we were headed east on an asphalt road that had been resurfaced that day. The signs along the road had been removed for some reason and there were no markings on the road itself.

We were behind a slow-moving car that had several people in it. Because the road had many small hills, I was exercising my patience by not passing even though there were no markings to tell me that it was unsafe to pass.

At last we came to a stretch that appeared to be level and straight and I pulled out to pass. As I speeded up and began to come alongside the other car, a command appeared in my consciousness. "Get back!"

What are your thoughts as you read this little story?

Michael Meier

I immediately applied brakes and ducked in behind the slower car. As I did so, another car, also full of people, suddenly appeared in the oncoming lane. We were close enough that I could see the very wide eyes of the driver as we passed.

There had been a small swale or valley that hid the oncoming car. The combination of new asphalt, the flat light of dusk and the lack of signs or markings had given me a false sense of security. I had been about one second from a head-on collision that very likely would have involved three cars and a great deal of death and serious injury.

Was I a hero? I was a second away from being the person responsible for the extinction of at least two and perhaps three families. I was certainly not a hero.

Did I save lives? I guess I did, but I have never doubted for a single moment that it was the direct intervention of God that saved those lives. I am forced to admit that I am not a person who simply obeys. I am a questioner.

Has God ever commanded you? What was your reaction?

What *Would* Jesus Do?

I have asked myself many times what it was about the command I received that caused me to obey without hesitation. I have learned to just accept that when one receives a command from God, obedience will come first and questions can wait.

There is no way to know on whose behalf God was working. He may have issued commands to all the drivers. It appeared that I was the only one who did anything but that may have been because I was the only one who was out of place. I don't know anything about the others involved or what they may have done since then to bring glory to God and His Kingdom. I do know that my son received his own command from God several years later.

In most cases, we don't even know when we have saved someone's life. I feel fortunate that some of those whose lives have been saved have at least recognized that something had been done for them.

God has shown me, and I am showing you that it is enough to simply accept the responsibility of a neighbor. We are living in God's Kingdom if we live our life as a neighbor to everyone we meet.

What's keeping you from loving your neighbor?

Michael Meier

When we notice something that needs to be done, and is within our capability, we step in and do it. We do not expect repayment. We don't even expect gratitude. We may expect, if we stop to think about it, that in our need someone will step forward as a neighbor. "Expect" probably isn't the correct word here because it holds the idea that we may feel disappointment if it doesn't happen.

"Faith" will be a better choice of words. In faith, we will not be disappointed. In faith we will supply reasons for our neighbors, assuming that they are unable, though willing, to act.

We may say then that the good neighbor acts in faith. When Jesus commanded his followers to love their neighbor as they loved themselves, he emphasized that loving God and loving one's neighbor are the foundation of all of the Jewish law—the foundation of everything important in the lives of those to whom he spoke.

What do you expect of your neighbor? Why?

5. Responsibility To Family

Jesus never married. What lessons can he teach me about living with a spouse?

He told his disciples to leave their homes, their fathers, mothers, brothers and sisters. How does this communicate a sense of responsibility?

Jesus left the clear message that a life–mine, yours, each person's–is to be measured in relation to its connection to God. The message that we should take from his relationship to the disciples, his brother, his mother, Mary Magdalene, Lazarus, Mary and Martha, the Samaritan woman, the woman taken in adultery, every sick, blind, lame, demented person who came to him for help, is that God is first.

How is family different than neighbor?

Michael Meier

Just as Jesus was loved by all of these people, you will be loved by the people in your life if/when you bring God to each and every relationship.

In many ways the family is more difficult to relate with than the others of the world. Why should this be? I believe that the answer is that our families expect things of us and we expect things of them.

The world's others don't even know we exist until we bump into them or smile at them or help them up or save their lives. Our family members, on the other hand, expect much of us.

It would be easy to resent those expectations if we didn't have them ourselves. Maybe it's too easy to resent them anyway. Many a relationship falls victim to resentment.

What do you expect of your family? Why?

What _Would_ Jesus Do?

A wife resents her husband's frequent or prolonged absences, his inability to participate in the everyday tasks of the family, his apparent self-centeredness, his failure to consult her on a matter that affects them both.

A husband resents his wife's relationship with the kids, her friendships, her insecurities and constant worries, her need to be in control.

Children resent their parents for spending time away from them. They resent their siblings for everything.

Even the best family must deal with flare-ups of resentment from time to time. We all tend to think that the other person, the other family has a better life than we do.

What would Jesus do in my family? He would see the needs of the wives and husbands, parents and children. Having seen the needs, He would respond by taking responsibility.

But he would not assume responsibility for anyone's happiness. He would be responsible for seeing and accepting. He would give gratitude and love to the other family members and to God.

Imagine Jesus in your family? Imagine that _you_ are Jesus in your family?

Michael Meier

He would join with them in communion—a communion based on the mutual seeking for the Kingdom of God and His righteousness.

Jesus would encourage the wife to let go of her expectations and simply love the man she married. He would gently ask the husband to release those small jealousies and just be grateful for the woman he married. He would bring the father and the mother together with the children to express their love and gratitude to each other and to God who made them and brought them together.

Having done this, He would turn their focus outward toward the world and ask them to love their neighbors as they have learned to love each other within the family.

Might you be the Way, the Truth and the Life for your family?

6. Responsibility To Ourselves

All this talk about loving others and being responsible for others. What about me?

What did Jesus do for himself?

Everything we know of Jesus' life from the gospel record tells us that he experienced no regret. What more could he do for himself? When I live my life as a "shining city on a hill" I, too will have no regrets.

I am my own worst enemy. I suspect that this is true of most, if not all people. It was no doubt equally true in the world that Jesus walked.

How do you love yourself? Is that the same love you give to the others in your life?

Michael Meier

Jesus must certainly have had this in mind when he summarized the law for that lawyer. As a student of human nature, he was certainly aware that the second part of the law could be problematic.

If I am critical of myself, if I have low self-esteem, if I fail to accept myself, what good then will it do to love my neighbor in this way?

It is interesting again to look at the whole story in the Gospel according to Matthew. Remember that the first part of the law was to love God with the entirety of one's being. This was the primary–the most important law and we can accept that. God is the origin of all and therefore deserves first place.

But, Jesus goes on, "the second is like unto it."

I encourage you to ask yourself, "How is loving my neighbor as I love myself like loving God with all of my heart and mind and strength?"

You can begin to understand the difficulties that are created when we pull passages out of their context. We're going to have to go back and really get to know Jesus before we can come up with an answer.

Do you love God above all else in your life? Could you?

What *Would* Jesus Do?

But first—I hope you agree that this question is an important one. There are several reasons to believe that it is. First, Jesus didn't engage in idle musings. Second, the gospel writers included this exchange and so it must have seemed important to them.

Finally, the Pharisees were baiting Jesus. They had selected one of their number, a lawyer, to trap Jesus into a heresy that would provide a basis for punishment. His words in these situations consistently demonstrate a wisdom that is astounding in its simplicity and truth.

With all of this weight behind the words, it is certainly appropriate for us to make sure we understand what Jesus had in mind.

Jesus was consistent in his message–particularly in his teachings to the disciples.

- Seek first the kingdom of God and His righteousness.

- I am the way, the truth and the life.

- Love one another as I have loved you.

Do you know any Pharisees? How do they make themselves known?

Michael Meier

- And Jesus loved him and said, "Go, and sell everything you have..."

- If you love your mother or father or sister or brother more than me, you are not worthy of me.

- No man has greater love than this–to lay down his life for those he loves.

- Love your enemies and pray for them.

The stories of the prodigal, the good Samaritan, the lost sheep, the laborers in the vineyard, the handmaidens waiting for the bridegroom, and all of the others–these parables had a consistent message and the message was (and is) that when we love we must not differentiate between the objects of our love.

Loving God, loving neighbors (even "enemies"), loving family, and loving self are all the same. If we do not love one, we are not loving any.

We must love ourselves in the same way that God loves us.

God loves _you_. What a marvelous work and a wonder you must be.

God loves me. What a marvelous work and a wonder I must be.

What a marvelous work and a wonder you are. What does that mean to you?

7. Possessions

Jesus demanded that the young prince get rid of everything he owned. How can I follow that example today?

Jesus lived a life without possessions. Is that possible today?

Go back again to the greatest of the laws. Love the Lord, God, with all your heart and soul and mind and strength and love your neighbor as yourself. God must be first and when put Him first, all worldly possessions lose their attraction.

God gives us things to steward. Stewardship is not the same thing as possession. Those things that God has given us are good. Clearly we can be grateful for those things and we should certainly enjoy them to the fullest.

What is first in your life? How is that working for you?

Michael Meier

Just as clearly, we can't allow these things–whether they are land, pets, herds, homes, machines, toys, natural resources or anything else that is of the world–to get between us and God or between us and our neighbor.

We may use things, appreciate things, create things, buy and sell things. We may have emotional attachments to things. The line is only drawn at love. We must put no thing, no possession, ahead of God (or our neighbor) in our love.

Stewardship is a word that is frequently misunderstood and misused. In our church community *stewardship* is used as a synonym for *giving*. *Giving* always refers to money.

Let's try to grasp what God had in mind when He gave man dominion over the birds and beasts and things of the earth. A present day example might be helpful.

What does stewardship mean to you?

What _Would_ Jesus Do?

In Amsterdam (and probably other Dutch cities) the bicycle is an extremely popular mode of transportation. Of course some could afford to buy and own a bicycle and others could not. Someone came up with the idea of spending tax (community) money to purchase some bicycles that would belong to everyone (or no one).

These bicycles were seeded around the city and anyone who needed to get from A to B could simply use one of these bicycles and leave it at the destination for the next person. Theft of bicycles was virtually eliminated in one magnificent act of stewardship.

Stewardship means *wise use*. The lessons of Jesus are most clear on this point. The servant who buried the money given into his keeping was rebuked as a poor steward. The landowner who built a second barn to hold the excess of his crop was used as an example of one who has his life's priorities wrong. To the one who has much, much will be given—but not to bury, to store, to hoard.

How could you better fulfill your role as steward?

Michael Meier

"The one who has much." Who is that person? Let me suggest that you can hold that person's hand anytime you want to. That person is the one who is grateful. That person is you and me.

When the rich young ruler begged Jesus to tell him what he must do to be saved, the advice of Jesus was to sell everything he had and give [the money] to the poor. For that young man, it was too steep a price to pay. I'm going to go out on a limb here and suggest that Jesus knew that the young prince wouldn't be able to let go of his possessions. Either way though, he would provide a wonderful lesson.

The early church described in the book of Acts seemingly took this literally and adopted a communal lifestyle as the most efficient in terms of material needs. They did, in fact, sell their possessions and used the money to help the poor and spread the good news.

What do you have that would be more valued to someone else? Why?

What *Would* Jesus Do?

The actions of the first generation Christians can also be viewed as an example of stewardship. I am certain that I possess things that others could put to use. If I relied on God to satisfy my needs and instead directed my heart and soul and mind and strength to use whatever comes to my hand to glorify God and bring His Kingdom to life for myself and my neighbors, would I be better off? Would my neighbors be better off?

There is an old saying, "The person has much who is grateful for what he has."

He has much who is grateful for what he has. What does that saying mean to you?

8. Wealth

Can wealth be good?

If it is easier for a camel to pass through the eye of the needle than for a rich man to enter heaven, should I avoid wealth?

Wealth for the sake of wealth is evidence that God is not first. On the other hand, God has made it clear that wealth is not evil by blessing his most faithful servants with it. If "more" is the rule by which we live, then God is not in the reckoning.

We have already discussed possessions, so let's restrict our discussion here to money. Trying to separate money from possessions probably wouldn't please most economists, but there are good reasons to make a distinction.

What use is money? What value has money?

What Would Jesus Do?

First, money has no intrinsic use. Its only utility lies in its ability to be easily converted to something else that does have utility. Yes, people have been known to burn paper money for warmth when they thought they would die otherwise. Coins have been used as decoration, as ballast, as replacement for a burned fuse, in numerous practical but temporary applications for which washers or stones would have been just as good. Money does not have value in the same way that a washing machine or a screwdriver has value.

Despite this, most of our lives are devoted to obtaining money. It seems we can never have too much money. In this respect, too, money is different than any other possession. No one accumulates washing machines or screwdrivers or, if they do, they may be viewed as eccentric. One who accumulates money is generally looked up to and seen as hard working, wise, worthy and capable. So money _is_ different from other things that we may possess.

What is your net worth?

Michael Meier

Money is even easier to accumulate because it is really only a symbol, an idea that we all agree about. It is possible to store up fantastic amounts of money without any boxes, or bags, or barns or silos. If I won the lottery, they wouldn't back a truck up to my door and unload bundles of currency. My next bank statement would simply show a very large deposit and my balance would suddenly be a big number.

Now, if I simply allowed that big number to show up every month and never changed anything about the way I live my life, the number would grow larger as time went by. If I did that, would I be any different than the landowner who, in the midst of planning how he would store his next crop, was summoned by God? Would I really be any different than the servant who buried the money entrusted to him?

What is your neighbor's net worth?

What *Would* Jesus Do?

Accumulation as an end cannot be justified. That is simply another name for greed. Jesus told us that it is foolish to build up treasure on earth. He gave us many examples to show that it is more than foolish–storing up those earthly riches changes the focus of our lives. We are so easily blinded by the idea of riches that we turn away from God and toward the money. "Show me the money!"

Why is it easier for a camel to go through the eye of a needle than for a rich man to enter the Kingdom of God? A little reflection produces this answer:

> *When a rich man speaks of putting his money to work, he is talking about making himself richer.*
>
> *When a man of God speaks of putting his money to work, he is speaking of building the Kingdom of God.*

God has no need of our money. His Kingdom has need of what our money can do.

How do you put your money to work?

9. A Challenge

I thought I had completed this handbook when my son made a comment that brought me up short. He had played golf in high school but now was planning to sell his golf clubs. He said that he could not play golf while people were going hungry. He said that Gandhi would not play golf. Jesus would not play golf.

I enjoy the game of golf and find it (usually) very relaxing. I pushed back a little, asking him why he believed that Jesus would not play golf. He said, "You tell me. You wrote the book."

Well, I felt somewhat uncomfortable. I had claimed to have written a handbook, using the spirit of Jesus to help people in their daily lives. If my claim is to be given credibility, shouldn't the handbook provide some guidance with a question like this?

How would you have answered?

What *Would* Jesus Do?

I just can't recall any guidance whatsoever in the Bible concerning the advisability of playing golf. I put the question on the back burner and let my subconscious work on it for a while. I prayed for guidance and I awaited an answer. No recognizable answer came. In the end, I came to the conclusion that the question has no real meaning.

Jesus (and Gandhi) lived life, drawing the maximum of joy from what God has provided. He lived as a child of God, accepting everything the Father offered and returning heartfelt thanks for it all. His mission and the mission he gave to us is simple, demanding and effective if we but carry it out.

1. Love God

2. Love each other

A third injunction may be inferred because it falls naturally from the two.

3. Do not let the love for anything else keep you from 1 and 2.

What was Jesus' calling? How did his actions reflect that calling?

Michael Meier

I simply cannot conceive that God wants everyone to be Mother Theresa. I thank God that Mother Theresa and others like her step forward, but if every one of us loved one another, there would be no need for Mother Theresas. If we each looked to our own mission, the poverty and ignorance and suffering that required Mother Theresa simply would not exist.

When God handed Jesus a bitter cup to drink, Jesus prayed that the cup might pass from Him. There was never a doubt that He would accept His Father's will and be grateful for the opportunity. All who would follow the example of Jesus must do likewise.

How would you apply Jesus' model to your own life?

What *Would* Jesus Do?

If my son is called to renounce the world and give himself completely to the poor and hungry, I would expect him to heed that call as he heeded his call to walk across the country in mid-winter. Until then, I would expect him to follow the example of Jesus, who simply *was* the Christ and live life, loving those he meets.

He struggles with these questions. He was ready to give up music for the same reasons. We counseled that the joy that he received from music (or golf) was what God intended.

God gives gifts for use in ministry and we don't always recognize them for what they are. The problems that arise do so because we believe we must do heroic deeds in ministry. All we can do and all we should do is use the gift or gifts we have been given to reach out to our new neighbors. Saving lives is most often simple and seldom heroic.

What gifts have been given to you that could be applied to nudging others toward the Kingdom?

10. Applications

But how can I apply all of this to my life?

Having accepted the challenge to apply the handbook to one issue, I felt compelled to provide applications for a few of the other issues that are dividing the Church today. I nearly said that the issues are dividing the Kingdom, but I realized that the Kingdom cannot be divided. If we *are* divided, it must be because we have not yet entered into the Kingdom.

You should notice that all of these applications seem very similar in the way they are structured. As I considered this, I came to understand the elaboration provided by Jesus when he said that "upon these hang all the laws and the prophets."

Where do you feel the need to apply Jesus to your life?
What prompted you to read this?

10.1. Homosexuality

"Christians" are making me feel like the worst of sinners. Why should I care what they think?

What does Jesus' life teach me about issues such as homosexuality?

Any speech or action that creates fear or separates one from another does not come from Christ and, by definition, is not Christian. I believe that Jesus would drive from the temple those who deal in fear and superiority.

The first step here is to separate the person from the act. It is not given to me or to you to define what is or is not sinful. It has been made abundantly clear that we are all sinners and that it is useless and destructive of love to concern ourselves with degree.

Doing or Being is what divides us. How do you see homosexuality? Why?

Michael Meier

I recognize that I am a sinner because of being human. I know, too, that you are sinner for the same reason. Beyond that, we are not free to feel superior for there can be no superiority where sin is concerned. We must love the person, making a neighbor of him or her.

Certainly God created male and female for a purpose and the institution of marriage was likewise ordained for a purpose.

It is difficult to find a study of homosexuality that is not biased from the outset.

It is possible that the homosexual person has been damaged in some way and that he or she is acting out of fear. It is equally likely that the anti-homosexual has been damaged in some way and is also acting out of fear. What is clear is that the tension between the two is causing disunity.

Neither do I condemn thee. Go and sin no more.

These are the words of Jesus to the woman taken in (the act of) adultery.

Judge not that ye be not judged.

Forgive us our trespasses as we forgive those who trespass against us.

Where do your attitudes about homosexuality come from?

What *Would* Jesus Do?

Jesus would certainly not condone any exclusionary action that prohibits us from freely sharing the gifts that we have received from God.

If we could only examine this issue dispassionately and in the light of prayer, we would see several things that would shed light.

- "Marriage" is a name for something. What's in a name? We don't change a thing by changing its name.

- What God blesses and what the government condones are two different things.

- We don't ask what our clergy do with their partners, nor do we base our opinion of them on the sex life they lead. In fact, we prefer not to think about that subject at all.

- Our churches are political organizations and behave as such.

- What does opinion have to do with God's Kingdom?

What is "marriage"? What does the Bible tell us about this relationship?

These are but a few of the ways we could think about homosexuality. These ways have the potential to be productive. Instead, we are spending our energy drawing lines to keep others out. We build walls of scriptural fragments, cemented with fear, that not only keep out others and their God-given gifts but also keep us in.

Fear is the best tool the world has for keeping us away from a relationship with God.

10.2. Abortion

Everything related to Homosexuality also relates to this issue. A woman (of whatever age) who finds herself pregnant will take one of two attitudes. Either she will experience joy at the new life inside her, or she will be fearful because she is not prepared for the experience.

What might cause a pregnant woman to be so fearful that she would choose abortion?

What *Would* Jesus Do?

Much of what is happening today with respect to abortion is politically motivated. God is not present in the fire-bombing of clinics or the murder of physicians just as He is not present in the procedure that removes the incipient life from the woman.

The woman who turns to the abortion clinic is already fearful, uncertain of the future and her place in it. She needs love and support. She needs to be told that God will love her no matter what.

She also needs to be told that the people in her life–her neighbors–will love her no matter what. Only when she has that assurance and feels secure in the fact that she is and will be loved will she be able to make a good decision. We must not give the message that she will be loved only if she does what we think is right.

People make poor decisions all the time and are forgiven. *We all do the best we know how and when we know better, we will do better.*‡

---

‡ I heard this on TV and the person who said it gave credit to someone else. I don't know who said it but he or she has a gift, which they shared with the rest of us.

What is the antidote for fear? How might it be applied here?

Michael Meier

When will we learn that we cannot dictate to others who they will be? People will be what God made them and do what they believe they must do. They will make that decision in the light of their knowledge, their ability, and their relationship with God.

What good does it do to label as illegal an act motivated by fear? The physician who performs the procedure is not a murderer. He or she is helping a fearful person to avoid being subjected to injury or death because of her fear. I do not believe that any physician wants to terminate a pregnancy. I believe that they accept that the pregnancy will be terminated with or without their help. They act to make sure that total injury is minimized.

Could we do a better job of removing the fear that causes a woman to seek an abortion? Of course we could. Will the government or any politically motivated group take that step? Certainly not. Political "progress" is made by creating fear and using it to move people in one direction or another.

It is up to you and to me to be a neighbor to that woman by showing her mercy. Her need is to be assured that she is loved and to make God part of her decision.

"Fear drives out reason." What lessons might we take from this piece of wisdom?

10.3. Poverty, Hunger, Disease

Jesus, who returned dead people to life, made blind people see, made crippled people walk and took from us the burden of our sins, could have cured all disease, poverty and hunger. God could do this today. Why then do we still struggle with them?

I knew a man once who was near death as a result of pancreatic cancer. He said that he had struggled with God when he first learned of the disease. He also said that he had come to realize that it was the greatest gift he had ever received.

When we stop trying to blame God and instead begin to give thanks to Him, then we will be ready to learn the meaning of these gifts.

What did Jesus do about hunger and poverty?

Michael Meier

When a hungry person refuses to come to the local food shelf or when a poverty-stricken mother allows her child to starve or die of cold or disease rather than ask for help, what is the lesson we learn?

When a family lives in their car rather than ask for help, what lesson do we learn?

When Mother Theresa assumes responsibility for providing compassion to those dying in poverty, what do we learn?

When a government punishes the <u>people</u> of another country for the actions of their <u>government</u>, what does the world learn?

God has given us a world to use and has built into it many opportunities for learning. Maybe we are an experiment. We have been given a roadmap and the basic rules and now it is up to us to follow the roadmap and live the rules.

When we don't, the result is poverty, hunger, disease–not necessarily for the one who failed to heed the rule–but for someone. We have become accustomed to assuming that our actions or inactions generate consequences that we–and only we–must bear.

What did Jesus do about disease?

What *Would* Jesus Do?

One day enough of us will see that we cause plagues of consequences for others of whom we may not even be aware. When this happens–when enough people are loving their neighbors–we will begin to see that poverty, disease and hunger will begin to recede from the world.

Reflect for a moment on the difference between "disease" and "diseased person".

11. The Way, The Truth, The Life

I am the Way, the Truth, and the Life. After all of this discussion, we come back to this statement. Without me, no one can go to the Father. If you had known me, you would have known the Father. But from now on, you do know him, and you have seen him.

It seems that our pursuit of what Jesus would *do* may have been a wild goose chase. All Jesus ever did—and all we should ever do—is *be* the truest reflection of the light that is God.

Jesus never had to make a decision about what to do. All that he did flowed directly from his being the Way, the Truth, the Life.

How is being the Way, Truth and Life in one situation an act of creation?

What *Would* Jesus Do?

Do you know that you and I are given the opportunity thousands of times each day to *be* the Way, the Truth, and the Life. Each time we choose that being, we create a new future of which we are part. That future comes into being at the moment we choose to let the Peace of God flow through us, reflect from us, and surround us. In that moment, it doesn't matter what we do. Whatever we do will bring peace.

The Kingdom of God, that place where Jesus lived and lives, is an endless succession of those moments of being the Way, the Truth, and the Life.

We stumble and lose focus. We find it so easy to fall out of being and into doing. The message of Jesus is that the stumbling doesn't matter. Here comes another decision for being, another chance to step out of doing, an opportunity to create a new future.

What would Jesus do? He would transcend doing—both his own and yours. He would connect with the part of you that is being a child of God. He would rejoice in that decision of yours and share his peace with you. He would spread his arms and welcome you into the Kingdom.

What would Jesus do? What would you do?

Can you be the Way, the Truth and the Life just for a moment?.

12. The Bottom Line

In all of this discussion of what Jesus would do, was there anything that surprised you? Jesus has been nothing if not consistent. Those who have read the gospels and who are familiar with the stories will have found no surprises here.

I lived most of my life on the outside of the Kingdom trying to look in. I was so frustrated by my inability to "get it." People occasionally asked me things like, "Are you a Christian?" They obviously meant something other than an inquiry about where I spent my Sunday mornings. I heard of "born again" Christians and never had any idea of what that event of being "born again" might be like.

Do we come to Jesus or does he come to us? Does it matter?

What *Would* Jesus Do?

I imagine myself to be like most people in those experiences. I saw a quote once to the effect that if a person couldn't remember when they came to Jesus, they probably hadn't.

I remember when, as a boy, I was fitted with eyeglasses for the first time. I had not had any feeling of need, but was caught during a screening at school. When I first stepped outside with those new glasses on, my world changed forever. I could never go back to what I now realized was a blurred world with no detail, no clarity.

That is a close as I can come to describing the moment when I said yes to Jesus. Through Jesus I was introduced to God and God has held me close to His heart ever since.

The way this happened was not due to any purpose of mine. It was as though I was caught in a routine screening for sinners and handed the correction.

In one instant my life changed and I will never be content to go back. "Born again" doesn't begin to describe what happened. I have no recollection of my entry into the world, so it was much more like being made alive for the first time.

Have you experienced a moment in which everyhing changed and you could never go back?

Michael Meier

It was my miracle.

Some of you reading this will understand perfectly what I am describing. Brothers and sisters, go now and spread the peace.

For the rest of you, be assured that this miracle happens thousands of times every day.

I pray that it will happen for you.

What would you give up in order to have everything made new in your life?

13. Origins

The Holy Bible is a wonderful book and it contains everything we should ever need to know about the mind of God and the faith journey of men and women. We should begin our journey in the Bible and we should end it there.

What continues to give me difficulty is something that has surely occurred to others but which I have never seen stated. The Bible was written by spiritually mature people. If you are anything like me, you don't have the maturity to fully appreciate the guidance that the Bible provides.

Why might the experiences of spiritually mature people be beyond our grasp?

Michael Meier

Our first encounter with the Bible may be tantalizing. Our intuition tells us that there is something there that we desperately need, but we can't grasp it. We pull out little bits and pieces that seem to ring true for us and we use them like a charm to ward off the demons that seem to be everywhere in our lives.

The more we read it, the more the Bible stories emerge as meaningful chunks. The people of the Bible begin to take form. We need to be able to relate to those people in order to fully appreciate the Bible's message.

Unfortunately, the Bible isn't about people–it's about God in relation to people. There isn't a single person in the Bible that we can say we know. Many novels have been written about biblical characters because people feel the need to supply characters that they can relate to in order to better understand their relationship with God.

At some point I realized that God didn't stop relating to people when the last New Testament book was committed to paper.

How is God relating to you today?

What *Would* Jesus Do?

God continued to relate to us throughout the centuries down to today. He is relating to you and to me at this very moment. What we must realize is that, while everything we need to know about relating to God is contained in the Bible, it may not be as clear to someone meeting God today for the first time.

Many people over the centuries since the ascension of Jesus have written of their experience of God. I'll go out on a limb and say that all are valid. Certainly there are radically different ways to experience God. We can see that from Noah, Abraham, Jacob, Joseph, Moses, Joshua, Ruth, Deborah, Job, David, Ezekiel, John the Baptist, Luke and John (to name but a few). Each of these without a doubt had at least one direct experience of God, but all told a different story.

Did someone share this book with you? There is a potential mentor or at least a partner.

Michael Meier

If we experience God differently, what is the Truth? It may be possible to arrive at the Truth by reading the Bible alone, but I have come to believe that the more we share our own faith journey and the more we seek to share the journey of others through reading, talking, meditation and prayer, the more we will appreciate and understand our own experience of God.

In the end, you will find that words are inadequate. "Understand" is so completely irrelevant as a way of relating to God that I am extremely reluctant to even use it here.

Philosophers speak of "the ineffable, " or that which is "non-sensible." God is so far beyond our understanding that we are incapable of experiencing "Him" directly. Read the last part of Job in which God responds to Job's questioning by saying, "Where were you ..."

I will hope for but not expect to experience God fully in this life. I am peaceful in the assurances that I will do so in the next life. Until then, the best I can do is to reflect on my own contacts with God and seek to enter into the contacts of others by experiencing them second-hand.

Do you know someone who could benefit from this message? You are a potential mentor.

What *Would* Jesus Do?

Latter-day experiences may be more accessible to us in terms of relating to conditions and outcomes. In other words, by reading about (for example) my experiences in the present time, you may find it easier to place yourself within the experience and use it to further develop your own relationship with God.

We all need a relationship with God. Some of us acknowledge the need and others are still denying it? Which group are you in?

Postscript

People who need this book will likely fall into two categories. One category includes those who might actually be asking themselves, "What <u>would</u> Jesus do?" and genuinely need to know an answer.

The second category includes those who are seeking, who do not know Jesus Christ but are interested in understanding the message that has so affected the world over the past two thousand years. This group includes many who are on the membership rolls of Christian congregations but who have made no genuine commitment to Christ.

How would you describe yourself?

An "other" category might include those who are merely curious or who are looking for hypocrisy so that they can justify remaining at arms length. I have made every effort to provide in this handbook something that can touch each of these classes of readers in the same way that Jesus, the master teacher, touched those with whom He came into contact.

If I have been effective, there is nothing in this book that will offend any denomination.

Of course denominations don't read books, people do. As humans we enjoy the ability to become offended at any time we choose. However, if the reader chooses to be offended, I make no apology because I have told here only what God (Father, Son and Holy Spirit) has placed into my heart.

God has been working on me for some time now—not ordering, not commanding, but not leaving me alone either. I knew I was supposed to write something, but just what it was supposed to be was not clear. It took an act of God in someone else's life to illuminate my task.

Have you been offended by something you found in this book? Do you understand why?

My son was a college student and one day, just before Christmas break, he was sitting in church on a Sunday morning when he was told to walk. He knew who was commanding him and he knew exactly what he was being commanded to do. He left the next day. He would have left right after church except that some of the people he talked with as he left persuaded him that he needed to make some minimal preparation.

He came home to tell us that he wouldn't be home for the holidays and to pick up a backpack and a few clothing items. He didn't take a shelter or sleeping bag, just a change of clothes and some extra socks. He walked from Ames, Iowa to Washington, D.C. over a period of 26 days to demonstrate the power of peace. The actual distance is more than 1000 miles, and he walked about 500 of those miles. He has told many people that he felt God's presence every step of the way. He had a warm place to sleep every night by the grace of God and the efforts of loving neighbors in Ames and across the country.

Have you had an experience like this? How long did you take to go into action?

On two occasions–once near the end of the second week, when his feet were covered with blisters and he couldn't face putting on his shoes one more time–God sent a snow storm that forced him to take a day of rest. Then he was needed in Indianapolis to be introduced in a church service and so was given a ride and a second day of healing. The second snowstorm came after ten more days of walking (30-40 miles each day).

This act was such a profound demonstration of faith that it caused me to examine again my own faith.

A few years ago Jim Ross, the pastor of our hometown church, offered a unique and wonderful spiritual experience to us one Sunday morning. Sally, my wife of 34 years accepted his invitation for both of us and I found myself in a situation I would not have chosen but which I desperately needed.

Jonathan, my son, was willing to listen to me talk about what had happened to me and use my experience as a springboard to his own.

What would it take for you to commit your life?

The many citizens of God's Kingdom with whom I have come into contact and with whom I can share my most profound feelings and thoughts—these people have shown me what I needed to share with everyone.

The last obstacle I had to face was the idea that anyone other than Jesus could offer him- or herself as the Way, The Truth and the Life. When I learned that none of us can do it consistently, but all of us can do it when necessary, I was ready to begin writing this handbook.

We are, together, the body of Christ. If we ask what Jesus would do with his body, we must find the answer in His soul. My readings and reflections assure me that Jesus Christ did not allow his body to be ruled by his mind but rather by his heart and soul. This handbook is for those who seek to know what is in the soul of Jesus, Son of Man and Son of God.

Seek and you will find. Knock and it will be opened to you.

Jesus will not be satisfied by an open door. He will rebuild you from the inside out. Are you prepared?

Questions for Discussion and Thought

1. What do you understand "faith" to mean?

2. How might we recognize that someone "has faith?"

3. How would you compare the faith of Jesus with that of Martin Luther King, Jr., Mother Theresa, M.K. Gandhi. George W. Bush, Oral Roberts, Robert Schuler, Billy Graham, yourself?

4. What does the future you are creating look like? What is your role in that future?

5. How do you understand your responsibility to yourself? What do you owe yourself?

6. What do you owe those closest to you? Who are you thinking of as you answer this question?

7. What should your neighbors expect of you?

8. Where do you draw the boundaries between neighbor, friend, family self?

9. How would Jesus respond to a person with cancer? With AIDS? With depression? With fear of being pregnant, giving birth, being responsible for a child?

10. If Jesus visited your church one Sunday, what would he find? How would he be welcomed? What would you expect of him?

11. Are you playing the part of Martha or of Mary.

12. Who is that person, apprehended in the act, caught red-handed, surrounded on all sides by judges and persecutors, who is told, *"Neither do I condemn you. Go, and sin no more."*

About The Author

Michael Meier is a fifty-something Minnesotan who grew up in Iowa and was born in South Dakota. He has spent time in Texas, California, Alaska, and Germany. He has been earning a living as a data manager in various industries, most recently healthcare. He met Jesus in 1997 after seeing Him around for more than 40 years and has been getting to know Him ever since. He believes that his experience will be useful to anyone else who might wish to meet Jesus and become friends with Him.

Lightning Source UK Ltd.
Milton Keynes UK
06 November 2010

162481UK00001B/53/A